The Amazon Fire TV Stick User Guide

2015 Edition

By

Charles Tulley

Table of Contents

Getting Started

Hardware Basics

Your Fire TV Stick is a complex device with a simple appearance. In fact, it's so simple, there's not even a power button, or anything except two connectors on it! The first connector is a micro USB port, into which you need to connect the micro USB cable that was included with the Fire TV Stick. The other connection is an HDMI connector, which you need to plug into your TV. As long as your TV has an HDMI port, you're set to go! We'll be covering the details of the setup of your Fire TV Stick in the next chapter of this book. Be sure to check the list below to ensure that everything that was supposed to arrive with your Fire TV stick was delivered.

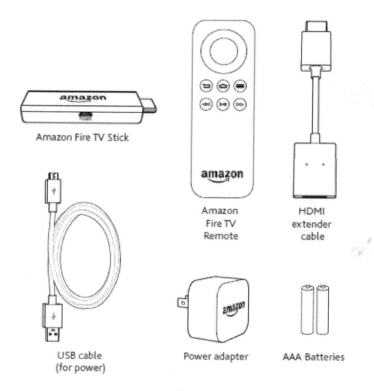

Amazon Fire TV Stick

Amazon
Fire TV
Remote

HDMI
extender
cable

USB cable
(for power)

Power adapter

AAA Batteries

The remote control for your Fire TV Stick is relatively simple as well. It has a total of twelve buttons, four of which are contained within a circular four-directional pad that you can use to navigate on your Fire TV Stick. When you see instructions to "scroll" in a particular direction, that means you should use the four-way directional pad to move that direction to find a particular menu item.

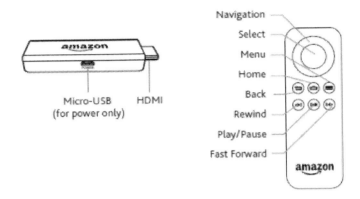

Your Fire TV Stick's remote comes with a pair of AAA batteries which you'll need to insert into the remote to power it up. On the back of the remote, there's a section which you can slide down to reveal the battery compartment Insert the batteries as shown on the internal diagram, and then re-attach the back of the remote control.

The remote that is included with the Fire TV Stick doesn't have voice search built in, but you can perform a voice search with the Fire TV app on your tablet or smartphone (more on this option later in this book), or, if you purchased a separate voice-enabled remote, follow the instructions below to use it.

To perform a voice search, press and hold the microphone button, speak the word or phrase you want to search for, and then release the button. Use the circular navigation pad to move up, down, left and right through the Fire TV Stick's menus. Press the round button in the center of the circular pad to select the item that you've highlighted on the screen. Use the Back button to move back one screen or menu. The Home button will take you to the main screen of your Fire TV Stick, no matter where you happen to be. The Menu button opens a contextual menu that varies based on what you currently have open on your Fire TV Stick. Rewind, play/pause and fast forward work like you would expect from a conventional video player, letting you rewind, alternate between play and pause and fast forward your media.

If you purchased an Amazon Fire Game Controller (sold separately from the Fire TV Stick, but used to play games and navigate through the Fire TV Stick's interface), it will also come with a pair of batteries (AA) which you can insert into the back of the device like you do with the remote control's batteries.

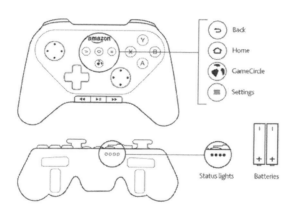

Your controller can operate like a second remote control for your Fire TV Stick, since it has many of the same buttons. In fact, the only thing it can't do like a voice-enabled remote is perform voice search, since there's no microphone built in to the controller. With back, home and menu (settings) buttons along with the control sticks and frontal rewind, play/pause and fast-forward buttons, though, you can navigate through the Fire TV Stick, play/pause media and perform just about all of the same tasks as you can with the remote. The end result is that the controller isn't just for gaming, and you don't have to put it down and pick up the remote when you want to switch from playing a game to watching a show or listening to some music.

Fire TV Stick Setup

Connecting your Fire TV Stick

Start by locating a free HDMI port on your television to which you can connect your Fire TV Stick. Note that the device comes with a short HDMI extender cable, which you can use in situations where you don't have enough room next to the HDMI port on your TV to directly connect the stick to the TV.

Plug your Fire TV Stick into the HDMI port on your TV, then connect one end of the micro USB cable to the device and connect the other end to the included power adapter. Plug this adapter into a wall outlet and you're ready to start the setup of your Fire TV Stick!

Device Setup

Once you power on the device, you'll see a brief splash screen with the Amazon logo, then you'll be asked to press the play/pause button on your remote, then you'll be asked to choose a network to connect to. Since the Fire TV Stick only has Wi-Fi and no Ethernet connection, you'll be presented with a list of Wi-Fi networks that the Fire TV Stick has detected in the area, like the one below:

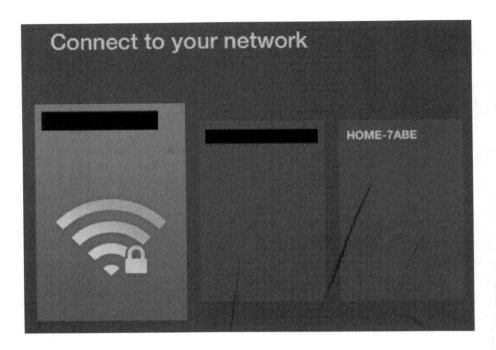

Use the left and right buttons on your remote's navigation circle to choose your Wi-Fi network, then press the select button. If your Wi-Fi network is secured (which is should be if it's not!), you'll need to enter in the password for the network.

Use the navigation wheel and the select button to enter letters. If you need to enter an uppercase letter, press the Menu button or select the **ABC** button on screen. If you need to enter symbols, select the **#$%** button on screen. Spaces are entered with the fast-forward button or the **Space** button on screen, and you can delete characters with the rewind or **DELETE** buttons. Once you've entered the password, select the **CONNECT** button or press the play/pause button on your remote control.

It may take a few moments to enter in the information, but if your network and password selections were correct, you'll see a message that you were able to successfully connect to the network. Awesome! That's *almost* all you need to do. But, depending on when and how you purchased/received your device, you may need to go through a quick device registration and/or wait for the device to download a system update. Don't worry; both of these steps are very easy and shouldn't take long to complete.

System Updates

Whenever your Fire TV Stick needs to perform a system update (as it likely may need to do when you first power it on), you'll be notified. In some cases, you'll have the option to accept the update, though in others the update will be applied automatically and your Fire TV Stick will be restarted. If you ever see a message like in the screen below, be sure not to cut the power to the Fire TV Stick off, otherwise you might break the device beyond repair (yep, it can be that serious).

Downloading the latest software

These system updates don't happen all that often, but when they do, it usually means that an exciting new feature is available for your Fire TV Stick! To perform a manual check for updates, start at the Home screen, then scroll down to Settings and over to System. Under the System sub-category, open the About section, then scroll down to **Check for System Update**. Select this option and your Fire TV Stick will perform a check to see if there is a new system update available to install.

Device Registration

If you purchased your Fire TV Stick directly from Amazon, it'll probably be pre-registered to your account automatically when you receive it. If you received it as a gift or purchased it from a third party, though, you'll need to go through the registration process. Since I purchased my Fire TV Stick from a 3rd party, I had to follow the registration process during the initial setup process.

From the registration page, choose the **Register** option (assuming you have an Amazon account already; if you don't, choose the **Create An Account** option and follow along with the instructions).

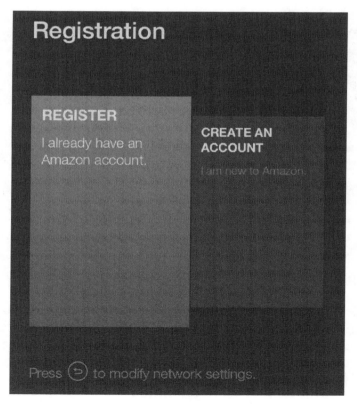

Next, use your remote to type in your email address, then select the **Next** option (or hit the play/pause button on your remote) and type in your password.

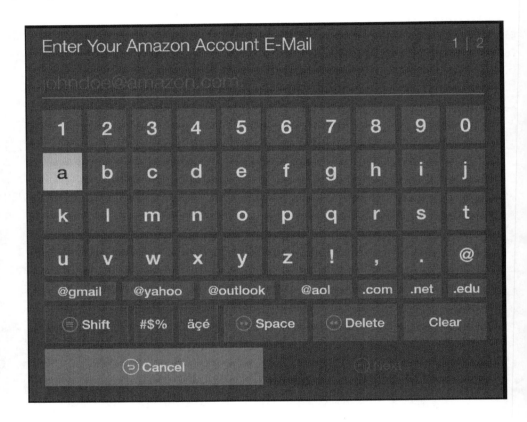

After you enter your password, select the **Sign In** option and your Fire TV Stick will connect to Amazon to register the device and verify your email and password information. If the registration is successful, you'll see a brief message to this effect, and then you'll be taken to a short video that introduces the Fire TV Stick to you before you're taken to the Fire TV Stick's Home screen. Note that you should watch this video carefully, as it explains a lot of valuable information about your Fire TV Stick (we'll be covering what's in the video and a whole lot more as we go through this book).

Audio Setup (HDMI/Optical Audio)

By default, your Fire TV Stick will come with Dolby Digital Plus set to "automatic," meaning that audio from the Fire TV Stick will in Dolby Digital Plug if your TV supports it, and in stereo quality if it doesn't. To change your audio setting once your Fire TV Stick is set up, go to the Home menu, then scroll all the way to the bottom and select **Settings**. From there, scroll all the way to the right until you reach the **Display & Sounds** section.

game

Open this section, and then scroll down to the **Audio** section. Select this section.

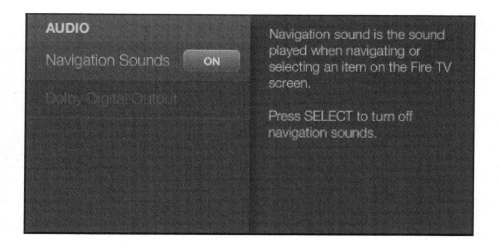

Scroll to the **Dolby Digital Output** section and select it.

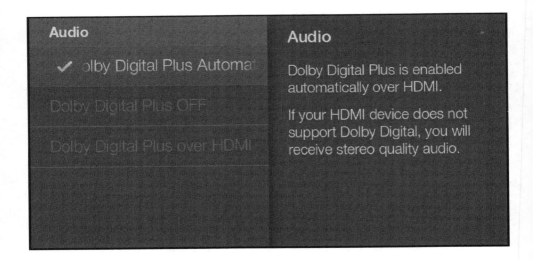

You'll note that the **Dolby Digital Plus Automatic** setting is selected. To choose a new setting, scroll to it and select it. You'll automatically be taken back to the previous menu once you make your selection. If you have trouble hearing audio after performing this step, simply change the setting back to **Dolby Digital Plus Automatic**.

Pairing a Remote/Controller

While the remote that comes with your Fire TV Stick is automatically paired with your Fire TV Stick when you insert the AAA batteries into the remote for the first time, if you've purchased a Game Controller or an alternative remote for your Fire TV Stick, you'll need to pair the devices with your Fire TV Stick in order to use them.

Starting at the Home screen, go to the Settings section, then scroll over and select the Controllers section.

Select either the **Amazon Fire TV Remotes** section or the **Bluetooth Game Controllers** section, depending on whether you want to pair a remote or a Game Controller. In either case, select the **Add New Remote** or **Add Bluetooth Controllers** option, then press and hold the Home button on your remote or Game Controller for at least five seconds. You'll be asked to confirm the pairing by selecting the remote or Controller from a list of found devices, then you'll need to wait a moment while the pairing process completes. After the Fire TV Stick discovers your remote or Game Controller, it will pair the device, and the device will be usable with your Fire TV Stick.

You can unpair remotes and Controllers by selecting them from the list of paired devices, then pressing the Menu button on the device to unpair it from the Fire TV Stick.

Navigation & Basic Use

Basic Navigation

With the help of the Fire TV Stick remote, navigation through all parts of the Fire TV Stick interface is a breeze.

The main user interface is composed of two sections. First, on the left, are the main categories. As you scroll through each category, the right-hand portion of the screen changes to reflect media, apps and other information that are relevant to that particular section.

For example, you can see that with the TV section selected, the right-hand portion now shows only TV shows, separated into a variety of categories. To explore a category in depth once it is selected, simply press right on the remote's circular navigation pad. You'll now be able to scroll up and down on the right-hand portion of the screen to explore the various sub-categories that Amazon has set up for you to view.

Continuing on with the TV category example, now that I've moved into the right-hand category, I can browse through subcategories like **Recently Added to Prime** (shows that were recently added to Amazon's Prime Instant Video collection), **Shop Latest TV** (new shows recently added that can be purchased), **Recommended TV** (shows that Amazon recommends based on your purchase and viewing history) and more.

NOTE: These categories change over time, and some may disappear and new ones may appear based on the changes that Amazon makes to the layout and structure of the Fire TV Stick's interface.

To move out of a subcategory or deeper into one, just press left or right on the navigation pad. As you move further into subcategories, more options will appear, such as the option to play the media, purchase media, open games/apps and more. We'll explore these options later in this book as we delve into the details of purchasing, viewing and playing media, apps and games.

Always remember: if you get lost, just press the **Home** button on your remote. This will take you back to the main menu, where you can start browsing through the categories and subcategories again. You can also use the **Back** button to move back a screen or menu, allowing you to back out of a category or subcategory slowly, one step at a time.

Main Menu Categories

At the time of writing, there are ten main categories on the Home screen. Let's go over what these are and what they're used for, briefly.

Search – While you can access Fire TV Stick's search at any time by holding down on the microphone button on the remote, this category lets you perform a text or voice search as well.

Home – Featuring an updated hodgepodge of information, this section shows you what apps/media/games you've recently accessed, recent videos that were added to Amazon Prime Instant Video, featured apps/media/games and more.

Prime Video – Contains TV and Movies that are all free to watch via an Amazon Prime subscription.

Movies – Free and premium movies are shown in this section, and you can browse through them and purchase or freely stream them from here.

TV – Want to watch TV shows? Here's where you can do it!

Watchlist – Movies and TV shows on Amazon can be added to your Watchlist, which is like a collection of bookmarks to let you keep track of what you really want to watch.

Video Library – If you've purchased or rented videos, they'll be in this section, allowing you easy access to them (and separating them from the other videos that are available for free streaming or to purchase).

Games – Amazon's poured a lot of their resources into developing games for the Fire TV Stick, and here's where you'll find a list of them that you've both purchased and that are available to buy or download.

Apps – All of the apps you've purchased or downloaded are shown here, and this is also where you'll be able to get more apps for your Fire TV Stick.

Music – If you've purchased music from Amazon, you can play it in this section. Note that as of late 2014, Prime Music is now available for play on both the Fire TV and the Fire TV Stick.

Photos – If you've uploaded photos into your Amazon Cloud Drive, they'll appear here, and you'll be able to browse through them or even use them as a "screensaver" for your TV when you're not using your Fire TV Stick for other activities.

Settings – We'll be going through this section in more detail later, but we've already seen a portion of this earlier, in the Setup section of the book when we talked about changing the audio output settings. There are lots more settings in this section, so if you want to change something about your Fire TV Stick, this is most likely where you'll be able to do it.

Voice Search

One of the most lauded features of the Fire TV, Voice Search is a powerful—but, more importantly, convenient—way to search for media in the Amazon ecosystem. Unfortunately, the remote that comes with the Fire TV Stick doesn't have a microphone built in. In order to use Voice Search, you'll either need to get a Fire TV remote with a microphone (purchasable from Amazon) or use the Fire TV app to perform a voice search.

Let's start by looking at how to use a remote with a microphone, then we'll talk about voice searching in the app. To get started with a voice search with a Fire TV remote with a microphone, just hold the remote up close to your mouth and press and hold the microphone button. Once you see the Voice Search page pop up, say what you want to search for!

When you're finished speaking, release the microphone button, and what you spoke will be analyzed, processed and a series of results will be displayed.

In this example, I was looking for the genre of "princess movies" for something my daughter wanted to watch, so I simply said "princess movies" in my voice search, and the search term both popped up and was automatically selected for me. Just select the search result that best matches what you said (there can be multiple search results in some cases) and you'll be taken to a search results page filled with media, apps and/or games that match your search results.

From the extensive testing I've performed, the voice search feature on the Fire TV Stick has some of the best voice recognition processing capabilities that I've ever seen. One way in which Voice Search is able to work so well is that it "learns" from the sound of your voice, by storing recordings of your searches in Amazon's cloud so that it can become better and better at processing what you say.

If you don't like the idea of your voice recordings being stored for a long period of time, you can periodically log into your Amazon account and delete them manually. First, log in to your Amazon account, then go to "Your Account." From there, look for a link that says "Manage Your Content and Devices."

Digital Content
Video, MP3 & Downloads

Digital Management
Manage Your Content and Devices
Manage Your Cloud Subscriptions
Your Amazon MP3 Settings
Your Video Library
Your Watchlist
Your Games and Software Library
Digital Gifts You Have Received
Your Apps and Devices
Amazon Instant Video Settings

Your Media Library
MP3 Downloads
Bonus Items
eDocs & Shorts
Your Collection

From here, click "Manage Your Devices" in the left column and then click on your Fire TV Stick device in the list of devices you own on the main portion of the screen. Finally, click "Manage voice recordings."

Fire TV Edit

Deregister
Manage voice recordings

A popup will appear, and you'll be given the option to delete the voice recordings, along with the warning that doing so may degrade your Voice Search experience. In my brief experience, deleting the recordings hasn't shown any ill effects, though your experience will most likely vary depending on the tone, accent and other unique characteristics of your voice.

The Amazon Fire TV App

As of late 2014, the Fire TV app is only available on Amazon and Android devices, but is expected to be released soon for Apple devices as well. To get started with the Fire TV app, download it from either the Google Play or Amazon app store and install it on your device. Once the app is downloaded and installed, open it, then ensure that your device's Wi-Fi is turned on and that you're connected to the same Wi-Fi network that your Fire TV Stick is connected to. When done correctly, this will enable your tablet or mobile device to see the Fire TV Stick on the network, allowing you to connect to it in the Fire TV app.

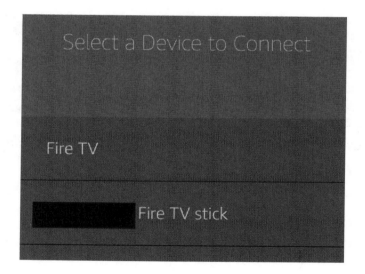

If you have more than one Fire TV or Fire TV Stick on the wireless network (which I do, as you can see above), select the device you wish to connect to. The first time you do this, your Fire TV Stick will show a 4-digit code that you'll need to enter into the Fire TV app in order to verify the connection of the app to the device.

Once the Fire TV app is connected to the Fire TV Stick, you can perform a voice search by pulling down on the microphone icon at the top, speaking while holding it down, and then releasing once you've finished talking into it.

So far, when testing this feature, I've run into a few issues where the connection between my phone and my Fire TV Stick has failed, resulting in a failed search that I've had to repeat. Most of the time, though, the search works properly, and brings up results on the Fire TV Stick just like was described in the previous section where we talked about voice searches with the microphone-enabled Fire TV remote.

The Fire TV app has more features than just voice search, though. You get access to a set of Home, Back, Menu, Rewind, Play/Pause and Fast Forward buttons on your tablet or mobile device, as well as a full keyboard which you can use to enter text on your Fire TV Stick when necessary.

To access the keyboard, tap the keyboard icon ( ) in the upper right of the app.

To access the full remote, pull up from the six dots near the bottom of the screen ( ).

To change which Fire TV device you want to connect to, tap the menu button in the upper left portion of the screen ( ).

Movies, Shows, Music & Photo Playback

Amazon Prime Instant Video

If you have an Amazon Prime subscription, you can watch a massive amount of movies and TV shows on your Fire TV Stick absolutely free. Amazon's Prime Instant Video is different than their Instant Video service, which allows you to rent and purchase movies and TV shows. You can easily identify Prime videos by the Prime logo in the upper left corner of the video image. This is particularly helpful when you are searching through videos, as it allows you to easily identify if the video you want to view will be free or whether you'll have to pay to see it.

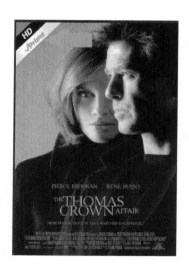

To quickly browse videos that are part of the Prime Instant Video collection, open the **Prime Video** section on the Home Menu. You can then browse through movies and TV shows that are in Prime that way. Or, if you prefer to browse both Prime and non-Prime movies and TV shows, start by choosing whether you want to watch Movies or TV shows, and then browse to that category on the Home screen.

While many new TV shows and movies are not added to the Prime Instant Video collection, there are a great many that are, and the collection continually grows larger as Amazon adds more media to the library. Be sure to check back in the **Recently Added to Prime** subcategories of the **Prime Video** category to see what new videos have been added!

Amazon Instant Video

Movies and TV shows that aren't part of the Prime Instant Video collection cost money to watch. You'll generally have two options when you want to watch a video from Amazon that isn't part of the Prime collection: Rent or Buy. Renting a video lets you watch it a set number of times over a set interval of time (once in two weeks, for example), so that you don't necessarily have to watch something you rent immediately after renting it. Purchasing a video, while more expensive than renting, lets you watch the video as many times as you want, and adds the video to your Video Library permanently.

Videos that you rent are also added to your Video Library, but only for the rental period, after which they are removed. Note that for some releases, there may not be an option to rent the video, and you may have to purchase it in order to view it. Also note that some videos are available in both standard definition and high definition (HD), the latter of which typically costs more to rent or purchase.

Whether you purchase or rent a video through your computer, tablet or Fire TV Stick, you'll be able to see it in your account across all of your devices, and you'll be able to view it just about anywhere as well. Amazon's Instant Videos use WhisperSync technology, so if you start watching a video on your Kindle HDX, for example, then stop it partway through and want to resume it on your Fire TV Stick, you'll be able to pick up watching it right where you left off.

Amazon says this about many of their rental videos (note that these terms may not apply to all rentals) as an explanation for the time period you have to watch the video:

> This rental video is available for 72 hours starting when you first play the video. When your order is complete, you have 30 days to begin the rental.
>
> You can Watch Now or Download the video to a compatible device. If you choose Watch Now, the video will instantly stream to your computer and you may later stream it on another compatible device. If you choose Download, you can download the video to a compatible device. This enables you to watch the video on that device without an Internet connection.
>
> Additional restrictions may apply. For more information, go to the Terms of Use.

Basically, what this means is that when you rent a video, you have 30 days to begin watching the video. Once you start watching it, though, you have 72 hours to finish watching it. After either of these deadlines expire, the rental will be removed from your video library and you'll have to pay to rent it again.

To get started renting or purchasing a video through your Fire TV Stick, first select which category you want to choose from. For this example, I'll rent a copy of Frozen from the Movies section of my Fire TV Stick. There are two ways to find the media you want: browsing or searching. In this case, I saw the movie previously as I was browsing through the **Shop New Release Movies** subcategory, so I'll find it that way.

Once you've found the movie you want to rent or purchase by scrolling left or right with the navigation pad, select it with the center select button on your remote.

This movie has a variety of options associated with it.

Rent HD $5.99	Buy HD $19.99	Add to Watchlist	Watch Trailer	More Ways to Watch

The rental option on the far left was the option selected by default. There's also an option to purchase the video to the right, then an option to add the video to your Watchlist (more on this at the end of this section), then an option to watch the trailer for the video, and finally, a **More Ways to Watch** option. Before renting an HD copy of the movie, let's see what the other ways to watch it are.

Remember when I mentioned that some videos have the option to rent or purchase both high definition and standard definition copies? Here's where you can make that choice, if you want. The less expensive SD options are listed under the **More Ways to Watch** section, while the HD options are displayed front and center on the video after you've selected it. For now, though, I'll just rent the HD version of this video, since I have an HD TV and I prefer the better resolution of HD videos. To back out of this popup menu, just press the back button on your remote.

Now that I'm back at the main screen, I'll select the **Rent** option. A popup window appears, asking me to confirm my rental of the video.

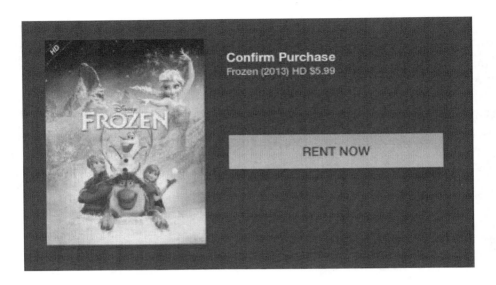

Hit the select button to confirm your rental, then wait a few seconds while the purchase is completed. Once it's done, if you're renting a video, you'll see a screen like this appear:

Selecting **WATCH NOW** will start your 72 hour viewing period, so if you don't want to watch your rental immediately, select **WATCH LATER**. Your video will be added to your video library, and you'll be able to start watching it within the next 30 days.

Note that if you purchase a video, you can watch it at any point, without time restrictions, so you don't need to worry about a 72 hour viewing period. Your purchase will still be added to your Video Library, and you can watch it at your leisure.

Third-Party Video Apps

Amazon Instant Video isn't the only service that's available on the Fire TV Stick. Netflix, Hulu Plus, Showtime Anytime, Bloomberg TV and other video apps are all available on the Fire TV Stick, with more services planned for the near and long-term future. If you're already a member of a service like Netflix, it's easy to get started watching videos from the service on your Fire TV Stick.

From the Home screen, go to the Apps section and browse through the library until you find the video app you want to install. Alternatively, if you know the name of the app, do a voice search on the app name. In this example, I'll search for and install Netflix on my Fire TV Stick, starting with a Voice Search for the app.

After selecting on the Voice Search result, I'm taking to a results list that includes both the app I'm looking for, as well as other apps, games and media that Amazon thinks are relevant to my search result.

Since the Netflix app is the first in the list, I just need to select it, and I'm then presented with the following screen.

From here, there are a few options and pieces of information to take note of.

First off, since the Netflix app is free, I can simply download it by selecting the **Download** option without spending any money or Amazon Coins (Amazon's virtual currency used for purchasing apps, games and in-app/game content). The next section over lets me view the details on the app. In this case, Netflix has a **Guidance Suggested** rating, which means that it may contain content not suitable for all ages.

This and other ratings are present on all of Amazon's apps and games, and are a good way to quickly find out if the app or game is suitable for the entire family. Selecting the option will give you more details on the rating, if any are available.

Finally, on the far right is the **Works With** section. Some apps and games require either the remote or Amazon Game Controller to operate, and which one (or both) is required will be displayed in this section.

On the left side, another menu is present, which you can browse to by scrolling to the far left with the navigation pad.

By scrolling up and down on this list, you can view details about the app (such as the version number, the description and so on), user reviews of the app written by other Amazon users and a list of apps that Amazon has marked as being similar in form or function to the app.

For now, though, all I want to do is download and install this third-party video app, so I'll scroll back up to the Overview section, highlight the **Download** option and select it.

The **Download** option will change to a **Downloading...** notification, which will in turn change to an **Open** option once the app is fully downloaded.

Select this option to open the app, and you're almost ready to go! If you're a subscriber to Netflix, you'll need to enter your email address and password in a similar manner as when you set up the Wi-Fi on your Fire TV Stick.

For the Netflix app, select the **Member sign in** option, then select the **Email** section and type in your email address, selecting the **Enter** option when you're done, and repeating the process for your **Password**. Remember to use the navigation pad to move up, down, left and right to highlight letters and numbers. Select the **!#$** key to switch from letters to symbols (then select the **abc** button to switch back).

While these instructions were specific for Netflix, this process will be virtually the same for other third-party video apps, especially if they require you to sign in through your member account. Other apps that don't require a sign in process will still need to be downloaded as outlined above.

Once an app is installed on your Fire TV Stick, it will show up in the **Apps** category under the **Your Apps Library** subcategory. This list (like the **Recent** subcategory in the **Home** category) is organized in descending order of app access time, so your most recently accessed apps will be displayed first. As you can see, since Netflix is the most recent app I installed, it shows up first on the list.

We'll cover this app installation process again when we talk about apps and games in general (and not just video apps in particular), as this search/browse/install procedure is the way in which you'll install all of your Fire TV Stick's apps and games.

Third-Party Music Apps

Music is also easy to listen to on your Fire TV Stick, thanks to the presence of music apps like Pandora, iHeartRadio and TuneIn radio. You can search for and install these apps just like you would any other app (as was outlined in the previous section). Some music apps may require that you register for an account or sign into them, while others may not, depending on what the app developer has decided to do.

Amazon Music Playback

As of late 2014, the Fire TV Stick is capable of playing both music that you've purchased and free streaming music that is available to Prime members through Amazon's Prime Music program. Huzzah! This feature took long enough to get here, but now that it is, we can start using it. Note that the introduction of Prime Music doesn't change the functionality of the Music section of the Fire TV Stick much at all, so the original instructions for this section are still included below for your reference. Before we cover that, though, let's look at what you'll need to do to listen to Prime Music on your Fire TV Stick.

First things first: you can't play Prime Music on your Fire TV Stick unless you add Prime Music to your music library from some other device. This other device can be a phone, PC or tablet. It's kind of annoying, yes, but as of December 2014, that's the situation as it stands. To add music to your library from Prime Music, go to www.amazon.com/primemusic or visit Prime Music on another device through an app, and then add Prime albums or Prime playlists to your library. Once these are in your library, you'll be able to play them on your Fire TV Stick.

To access Prime Music on your Fire TV Stick, go to the Music section of the Home Screen, then select **Your Prime Playlists** or open a Prime Album in the **Your Albums** section. Once that's done, just follow the directions below for browsing, playback and control options. That's really all there is to it!

Now that you know how to get Prime Music on your Fire TV Stick, let's take a close look at the **Music** section of the Home screen.

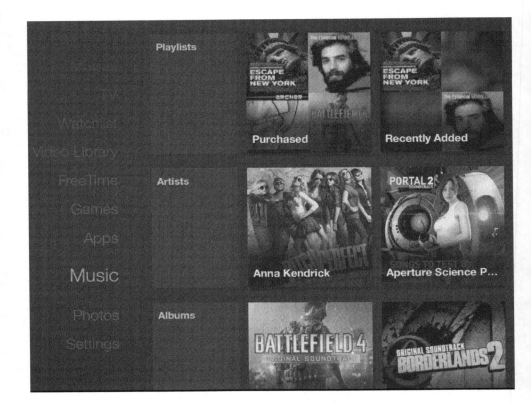

An overview of the Music section gives you a good idea of what you can do in it, and unsurprisingly, it's similar to other sections, such as Movies and TV Shows. I can view my music by playlists, artists, albums or genres, and scroll through the music in my library just like I can browse through the Movies and TV Shows sections.

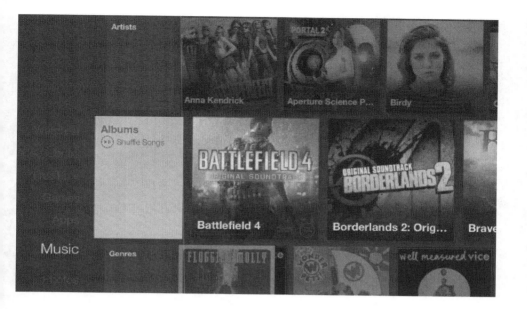

For example, by entering the Albums section, I can see the twelve albums to which my meager music collection belongs to. From this scrolling menu I can choose to either open the main category and play individual songs or use the **Play Album** or **Shuffle Album** shortcuts to quickly get the music going. (Similar shortcuts exist for the Genres and Artists scrolling views as well.)

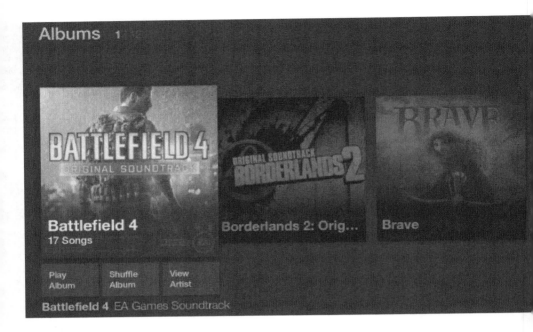

Pressing left, right, up and down on the selector wheel allows me to choose which individual songs I want to play, or choose the **All Songs** option in this example where I browsed through my music library using the **Album** view and then dug down deeper into the album details.

You can skip back and forward through songs using the back and forward buttons on your remote control, and you can pause and resume playback with the play/pause button.

Amazon Cloud Drive Photo Viewing

Photos that you take on your Kindle Fire HDX or that you upload to your Cloud Drive through the Cloud Drive app for iOS or Android (which you can get at amazon.com/clouddriveapp) will appear in the **Photos** section of the Home screen.

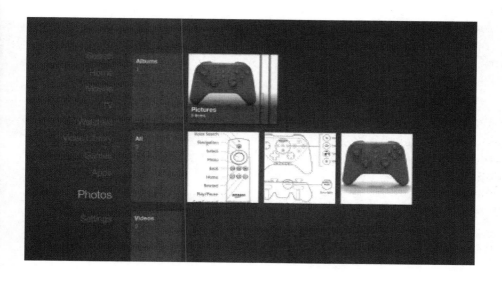

You'll notice that the only photos I've uploaded to my Cloud Drive directory thus far are some Fire TV Stick controller and remote schematics and images. As I add photos and delete them through the Cloud Drive app on my computer or phone, they are added and deleted with only a few seconds worth of a delay in the Fire TV Stick's Photos section.

If you browse through your photos, you'll notice that a couple of options may appear.

Selecting the **Start Slideshow** option (which appears when you're viewing photo albums) will start a slideshow based on the currently selected album you are viewing. You can also set an album as a screen saver with the second option. The Screen Saver is activated when your Fire TV Stick is left unused for several minutes, and plays for a short time before the screen goes dark. To resume where you left off after the screen saver or dark screen appears, just hit any button on your remote or Game Controller.

By default, if you don't have any photos uploaded for the Fire TV Stick to use as a screen saver, it will display a collection of landscape photos as screen saver images. To learn how to view and change your screen saver settings, check out the Advanced Settings sub-section of this guide book's Fire TV Stick Settings chapter.

Playing Games, Using Apps & Amazon Coins

Amazon Fire Game Controller

The Amazon Game Controller is a special controller built specifically for the Fire TV and Fire TV Stick. We covered the remote-specific functions of this controller earlier in the **Getting Started** section, but let's talk about the game-specific functions of the controller now.

(Real quick, though, be aware that while the Fire TV is capable of playing a wide range of games available on the Amazon app store, the Fire TV Stick is more limited in what it can do, simply because it doesn't have the same processing power as the Fire TV does. That's okay, though, because you can still play lots of games, just not ones that have a lot of fancy graphics or require the Fire TV's hardware to run.)

In addition to the buttons and control sticks you see on the top of the controller, there are two buttons and two triggers on the back of the controller that you can operate with your index fingers. The buttons, triggers and control sticks on the Game Controller will all be used in different ways depending on the game you play, but you don't have to worry about figuring out the controls before you play a game for the first time. Each game you purchase will have instructions or a tutorial at the beginning, explaining the controls to you, and instructing you in how to use the Game Controller to play the game.

Remember: although the Game Controller is primarily for games, it can also be used to navigate your Fire TV Stick's menus and play media. For more on these functions, see the **Getting Started** section at the beginning of this book.

Getting Games & Apps

Games and Apps can be downloaded from their respective sections on the Home menu. To get started, choose a section (I'll be purchasing a game called Rayman Fiesta Run for this example), such as Games. You can browse to find the app or game you want to install, or you can perform a Voice Search instead.

To start, I'll scroll down to the **Games** category and then scroll to the **Categories** sub-category of the Games section. I feel like playing an Adventure game, so I'll scroll over to the **Adventure** section and select it, then begin browsing through the games in this section.

Now that I've found a game I want to play, I'll select it, bringing up a screen that's very similar to the one we saw in an earlier section of this book when we covered the installation of the free Netflix app.

As with the Netflix app purchase and the rental of the movie that we covered earlier, purchasing a game or an app has the same basic options and information.

Buy $2.99 or 299 Coins	You have 1,007 Coins	Key Details In-App Purchasing GameCircle	Works With Game Controller

The first option will allow you to purchase the game or app (or download it for free, if the game or app doesn't have a price on it). The next option, when selected, gives you the option to purchase Amazon Coins (more on these at the end of this section). The next section gives you more details about the game/app and what features it possesses. Finally, the last section tells you what the game/app supports for controls, either the Fire TV Stick's remote or an Amazon Game Controller (sold separately from the Fire TV Stick).

Selecting the **Buy** option will show a popup like the one you see above. Apps and games can be purchased with either real money or with Amazon's virtual "Coin" currency. In this case, since I have enough coins available, I purchased the game with Coins. Pay special attention to the Notice at the top of the popup, detailing that the app/game I'm about to purchase requires a Game Controller to operate. If you don't have a Game Controller, don't purchase apps or games that require one, since you won't be able to operate them.

After you purchase your game or app, it will download to your Fire TV Stick, and you'll then be able to open it. In some cases, you may see something like this appear when you go to open a newly acquired or updated app or game:

Some games and apps (such as games with HD graphics or apps with large amounts of content) require additional downloads after purchase. These downloads can take a few minutes to process, and you'll be able to use your game/app once the download is complete.

Amazon GameCircle

When you start playing games, you may notice that you're prompted to change your GameCircle profile in a popup like this one:

So, what is GameCircle? It's a service provided by Amazon that—for supported games—tracks your game progress, lets you compare your scores to others and lets you sync your progress in a game to the cloud so you don't have to start the game over again should something happen to the local copy of the game. A complete list of games that have enabled GameCircle is available right here on Amazon.com.

Press the **Menu** button on your controller or remote, and you'll see a screen like this one:

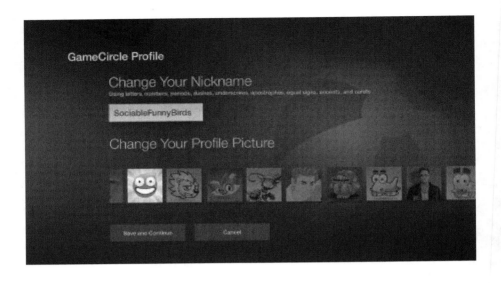

From this screen, you can change your GameCircle nickname and choose a profile picture from one of the predefined options. This nickname and profile picture will be displayed next to your score on leaderboards for games that have GameCircle enabled.

Amazon Coins

Back in 2013, Amazon introduced Amazon Coins. Amazon Coins are an Amazon-only virtual currency that you can use to purchase games, apps and in-game/in-app content. 100 Amazon coins are worth $1, but the larger quantity of coins you purchase, the more real-world money you save (for example, 500 coins can cost $4.80, but 10,000 coins can cost $90.00). The downside of coins, of course, is that if you don't use them, you lose out on the money you spent on them, since you can't transfer your Amazon Coins back into cash. The upside is that if you purchase lots of games, apps or in-game/in-app content, Amazon Coins can help you save up to 10% off of what you would pay if you purchased said content with real-world money. Amazon Coins also "never expire" according to Amazon, so you can use them quickly or slowly depending on what you want to do.

Sideloading Apps on the Fire TV Stick

What is Sideloading?

"Sideloading" is a term used to describe the act of installing apps onto a device (such as the Fire TV Stick) without going through an official app store (such as the Amazon Appstore). Since the Fire TV Stick is an Android-based device, you can sideload apps onto it just like you can on other Android-based devices, like phones and tablets. Before you start the process of sideloading an app onto your Fire TV Stick, there are a few things that are important for you to know.

First, this process is somewhat technical, and requires that you download and install third-party software onto your computer, and then run said software from a command line. All of the examples in this book will be given from the perspective of a Windows computer, though the instructions are easily adapted to other operating systems, though you may have to do some extra research on your own to do so.

Second, sideloading doesn't guarantee that the app you're loading onto your Fire TV Stick will actually work. The Fire TV Stick is different from other Android devices in that it has no touchscreen on it, so a lot of apps won't work properly (or at all) because of this (and because of other differences between the Fire TV Stick and a more standard tablet/phone-based device). For example, I have personally tested over a dozen browsers, and only one (FlashFox) works at all on the Fire TV Stick, and even when it works, the controls refuse to operate correctly so much that it's next to useless to try and use it. App developers who create apps for the Fire TV Stick have to adjust their existing apps to support the controller/remote control scheme of the Fire TV Stick, which is something that standard Android apps don't have to worry about.

Finally, while the sideloading process isn't super complex and the danger of doing something wrong is low, keep in mind that there still exists the remote possibility that you could potentially damage your Fire TV Stick or your computer during this process. Based on the research and testing I've put into documenting the sideloading procedure, I rate the possibility of something going wrong as "very very low" but it still exists nonetheless.

How to Sideload Apps on your Fire TV Stick

Step 1: Enable ADB (Android Debug Bridge) Debugging

Note: This is a step that should only have to be performed the first time you go to sideload an app and shouldn't need to be repeated unless you reset your Fire TV Stick to factory default settings.

ADB stands for Android Debug Bridge, something that allows developers gain direct access to an Android device so they can load and debug apps that they develop for the device. Since the Fire TV Stick is an Android device, you can (and need to) enable this option so that you can sideload apps onto the Fire TV Stick.

Starting from your Fire TV Stick's Home screen, scroll down to the Settings section, then scroll across to the System section. Select the System section and scroll down and select Developer Options.

Select the top option in the list (ADB debugging) to turn it on, then turn the second option in the list (Allow Apps from Unknown Sources) on and then press the back button once to return to the System menu.

Step 2: Find Your Fire TV Stick's IP Address

Note: This is a step that should only have to be performed the first time you go to sideload an app. If you find that subsequent steps in the sideloading process are failing at a later point in time, though, it's a good idea to check the IP Address again, just in case it has changed since the last time you sideloaded.

From the System menu, scroll up until you reach the About section, then select to open it. You should see something like this appear under the Network section:

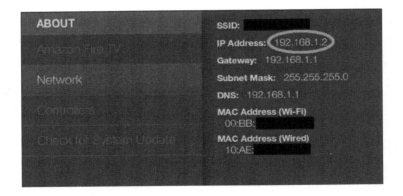

Take note of the IP Address shown in this section (the IP of my Fire TV Stick is 192.168.1.2) since you'll need that in just a little while.

Step 3: Install ADB (Android Debug Bridge) on Your Computer

Now that you have the relevant information gathered from your Fire TV Stick, it's time to turn the attention back to your computer. In order for your computer to be able to communicate with the Fire TV Stick, the ADB software has to be installed on your computer. To help keep this section as fresh as possible, I'm going to direct you **to this link: http://appsna.gr/1218**, which is brought to you by the folks over at AppSnagr, who I've worked with before. They've promised to keep that link updated as they root out new and easier ways to get ADB loaded onto your computer.

Once you have ADB installed, you're just about ready to connect to your Fire TV Stick to start sideloading apps!

Step 4: Connect to Your Fire TV Stick via ADB on Your Computer

To perform the actual connection process that lets your computer talk to your Fire TV Stick, you'll first need to make sure that both your computer and your Fire TV Stick are connected to the same network. I run a fairly complex set of networks at my home and office, so it's a bit more complicated for me to connect my computer to my Fire TV Stick than it will be for most folks. The rule of thumb you should follow is to make sure that both the Fire TV Stick and your computer are connected to the same router/modem so that they can talk to each other through this device.

Start by opening a command prompt (or, if you're on a Mac or Linux machine, a Terminal) on Windows by pressing the **Windows** key and the **R** key together to open the **Run** box. Type **cmd** into the Run box and then press enter, and you'll see a black box appear on your screen. This is the **Command Prompt**, a command-line-only tool for your computer. This is how you'll interact with the ADB program, which is what we'll do in the next step.

Before you can use the ADB program, you'll need to navigate to the folder where it's installed. You can do this on Windows by typing **cd x:\location\of\adb\program** and pressing **Enter**, like you see below. In the example below, I installed ADB to **c:\adb** so I just have to **cd** (or "change directory") to that folder. The command on Mac and Linux systems (**cd**) is the same on Windows.

Now that you're in the ADB folder where the **adb.exe** program is located (or the equivalent program on your Mac/Linux system), you need to start the **ADB daemon**, a small program that needs to run in the background. Do this by typing **adb kill-server** and pressing **Enter** and then type **adb start-server** and press **Enter**. If successful, you should see a message like the following appear. Note that if you don't type **adb kill-server** before issuing the start-server command, things may not work properly, especially if you've got an old ADB daemon instance running from a previous sideload excursion.

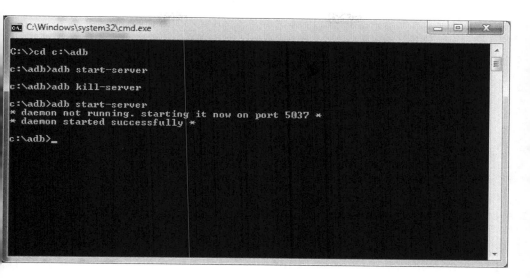

Now that the ADB daemon is running, it's time to connect to the Fire TV Stick. Do this by typing **adb connect x.x.x.x** where **x.x.x.x** is the IP Address of your Fire TV Stick that you noted earlier in this guide.

Now that your computer is connected to your Fire TV Stick, you're ready to move on to the next step: sideloading apps onto your Fire TV Stick!

Step 5: Install Your App on your Fire TV Stick

Now that your computer is talking to your Fire TV Stick over the local network courtesy of the ADB program, it's time for the big finale: installing your app! Before you can install the app, you'll need a copy of its installation program, something called an .APK file, which you can download from numerous sources on the web. For a few places that I like to get .APK files for apps, you can take a look at the last chapter in this book. Regardless of which app you download, be sure to only download and install legally-obtained apps on your Fire TV Stick. Also remember that many apps won't work properly on the Fire TV Stick, but that's okay! It's easy to install and uninstall them if they don't work out.

Once you have an .APK file downloaded, make note of its location on your computer. For this example, I downloaded the FlashFox browser to the root (c:\) drive of my computer. After you've connected to your Fire TV Stick with the **adb connect** command, you can use the **adb install apkfile.apk** command to install an .APK file, as seen in the following example. Note that unless the .APK file is in the same directory/folder as the adb.exe (or Mac/Linux equivalent), you'll need to include the full file path to the .APK file.

The command may take a few moments to execute (I've seen it take as long as 2 minutes but your time may vary depending on the size of the .APK and the speed of your network), but once it's done, you should see a **Success** message.

That's it! Yes, that's really all there is to it! Now all you need to do is check and see if the sideloaded app you just installed works on the Fire TV Stick.

Step 6: Accessing, Modifying & Uninstalling Sideloaded Apps on Your Fire TV Stick

So you have your app installed on your Fire TV Stick, but when you go to the Home screen to find it... it's not there? What??

Well, it turns out that Amazon restricts what apps can appear on the Home screen, and any apps that are sideloaded onto your Fire TV Stick will require a few extra steps to access. This is disappointing, but there's no way around it (and this is according to official Amazon documentation).

To access sideloaded apps, you'll need to scroll down on the Home screen to Settings, then over to the Applications section.

From inside the Applications section, just scroll down through it until you see the name of the application that you loaded onto your Fire TV Stick and then select it. You'll see a popup appear like the following one:

Select the **Launch application** option to open the app, and you're ready to go!

If you ever need to close an app that's misbehaving (frozen, won't respond, or is taking up a lot of system resources), you can select the **Force stop** option to force the app to close immediately.

To uninstall a sideloaded (or regularly installed) app, select the **Uninstall** option. There's also a way to do this via command line from your computer, but it requires that you know the technical "package name" of the app, so it's best to do it from the Fire TV Stick itself. If you're curious, the command line option is **adb uninstall full.package.name**. You can get a full list of the apps installed on your Fire TV Stick from the command line by running the **adb shell pm list packages –f** command, which also gives you the full package names of the apps installed.

If you want to clear all of the data that a particular app has saved, select the **Clear data** option, and if you just want to clear any cached data that an app is storing on the Fire TV Stick, select the **Clear cache** option.

Step 7: Finding Apps to Sideload Onto Your Fire TV Stick

In my testing, I've found that some of the more popular apps to sideload (like the Dolphin Browser, for example) don't work on the Fire TV Stick simply because of the differences the Fire TV Stick has from a conventional Android device. You'll have to experiment with different app installs to find ones that work, as well as work through the quirks of each app you install.

Remember: if an app gets stuck or hung, you can always use either the Home button on your remote/controller, or you can reset the Fire TV Stick by unplugging it and then plugging it back in. You should expect to run into a few instances where apps crash, hang or otherwise don't behave properly during your sideloading adventures.

Also remember that directly downloading and installing apps onto your Fire TV Stick or other Android devices without using an official market/appstore could cause your Android or PC device to become infected with malware. It's not unheard of for websites or even apps themselves to be infected with software designed to harm your computer, Android device or try and steal personal information. Be sure to have a good virus scanner installed on your computer (which you should have installed anyway) and **use an overabundance of caution when downloading and installing .APK files from unknown or unofficial sources.**

With that in mind, one of the places I like to look for apps to download is AppsApk. While I'm not affiliated with them in any way, they do appear to have a good selection of legal freeware apps that don't violate copyright, and their site (at the time of this writing) is laid out in a way that appears to actively fight against software piracy and illegally downloaded apps. You'll need to do some due diligence on this matter yourself, though, as with any site you visit.

Another good way to find .APK files to download is to search on Google or another search engine for **APK download *appname*** where "*appname*" is the name, genre or type of app you're looking for.

Again, please respect copyrights and don't pirate apps or other software.

Fire TV Stick Settings

Advanced Settings

As of the Fire TV Stick's launch, there are a total of seven sections in the Home screen's **Settings** section. We'll go through all of these briefly, then touch on a few of the most important ones in detail, including those that you're most likely to use at some point in your Fire TV Stick's life.

Display & Sounds

Here's where you can adjust the display and sound settings for your Fire TV Stick, including Dolby sound and the video settings.

Parental Controls

We'll talk more about Parental Controls in detail later in this section. For now, though, this is where you'll go to enable, disable and configure Parental Controls on your Fire TV Stick.

Controllers

Here you can pair and unpair remote controls and Game Controllers to and from your Fire TV Stick, which was covered in an earlier section of this guide book.

Applications

While most people won't need to worry about this section, if you ever need or want to change settings for specific applications installed on your Fire TV Stick, here is where you can do it.

System

The System section gives you access to all of the detailed system settings. Except for the factory default reset section, most folks won't need to access this section, but we'll go over the various options in this section in a little more detail later in this section of the guide book.

Help

Looking for Amazon-provided help videos, tips on the most common questions about the Fire TV Stick or do you want Amazon to call you while you're on your Fire TV Stick and help you with any issues you might be having? This is the place to go for any unanswered questions!

My Account

This is where you'll find the deregistration option for your Fire TV Stick (covered in detail later in this section) as well as the option to perform a manual synchronization of your Amazon content. Use this option if you see that your Fire TV Stick isn't up to date with your latest app, game or media purchases.

Parental Controls

Setting up parental controls on your Fire TV Stick allows you to lock certain sections of the Fire TV Stick behind a 5-digit PIN. To set up parental controls, start from the Home screen and go to the Settings section, then scroll right until you reach Parental Controls. Open this section, then select the only option currently available to you.

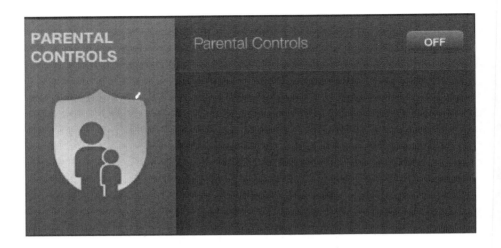

Selecting the **Parental Controls OFF** option will turn parental controls on, prompting you to enter an 5-digit PIN two times in a row.

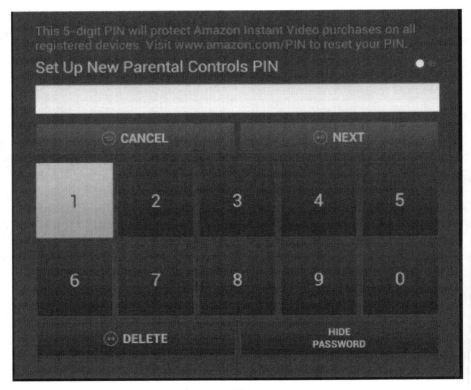

Once you've entered and confirmed your PIN, you'll see several new options on the Parental Controls section. We'll outline these below.

Parental Controls – Select this to turn parental controls on and off. Note that this action requires the entry of your PIN.

PIN Protect Purchases – Turning this setting on will require the entry of your PIN before any purchases can be made on your Fire TV Stick.

PIN Protect Amazon Video – Turning this setting on will require the entry of your PIN before any Amazon Instant Video purchases can be made (other purchases, however, can still be made without requiring the entry of the PIN).

Block Content Types – Use this section to block games and apps or photos from being used/viewed without first entering the PIN.

Change PIN – If you want to change your PIN, select this, enter your old PIN, then enter your new PIN two times.

Note that if you forget your PIN, you can visit amazon.com/PIN to reset it.

Amazon FreeTime

FreeTime is one of the major areas where the Fire TV Stick (currently) falls short of its big brother, the Fire TV. Upon its initial release (this may change later, of course), the Fire TV Stick did not include FreeTime, and thus the advanced parental controls and granular media filtering options are not available on the Fire TV Stick.

Factory Default Reset

If you ever want to sell your Fire TV Stick, or you're getting rid of it for some other reason, it's a good idea to perform a Factory Default reset on it. Resetting the device back to its factory default settings will get rid of all of your personal information on the device, helping to secure things like your login information and your personal preferences. Note that performing this factory default reset will result in the loss of all of your personal information on the Fire TV Stick. If you perform this step, you'll need to re-register the Fire TV Stick in order to use it under your account again.

To perform a Factory Default reset, start at the Home screen and scroll down to the Settings section. From there, scroll right, all the way into the System section. Select the System section, then scroll all the way down to the bottom, and select the Reset to Factory Default option.

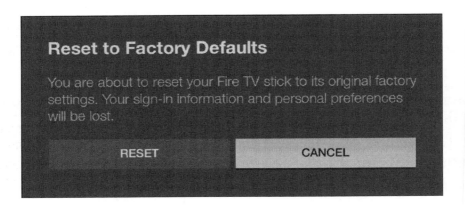

Select the **RESET** option and confirm that you want to reset the Fire TV Stick back to its default settings.

The factory default reset can take a few minutes, and your Fire TV Stick may reboot one or more times during the process. At the end of it, though, when the Fire TV Stick starts back up, you'll be prompted to start the setup process of the device yet again, starting with the setup of the Internet connection.

Note that if your device was pre-registered to your Amazon account when you purchased it and you perform a factory default reset, you'll have to manually register the device as was covered in a separate section of this guide.

Deregister Your Fire TV Stick

Deregistration of your Fire TV Stick is similar to performing a factory default reset, but may not result in the same level of privacy protection. Deregistration is best performed in situations where you want to, for example, switch your Fire TV Stick from your spouse's Amazon account to your own, or where you otherwise know and trust the person whose account you are switching the Fire TV Stick to.

Deregistration will remove any of your purchased apps, games and media from the device, and the apps, media and games from the new account that you register the Fire TV Stick to will appear instead. You can, of course, re-register the Fire TV Stick under the same account that you had on it before the deregistration process as well.

To perform a deregistration of your Fire TV Stick, start from the Home screen and scroll down to the Settings section. From there, scroll to the right until you reach the My Account section. Select this section, then select the Amazon Account section (which should be the first selection in the list). You'll see a screen like this appear, with the single option to deregister your Fire TV Stick.

Amazon Account

Deregister

Your Fire TV stick will be deregistered from your Amazon account. This will remove content from your device and many features will not work. After deregistering, you can register your Fire TV stick to another Amazon account.

If you don't want to deregister your Fire TV Stick, press the back button on your remote. If you wish to proceed, select the option displayed. You'll be asked to confirm this action, and once you confirm, you'll be taken to a registration page where you'll need to enter your Amazon email address and password to associate the Fire TV Stick with your account again. Details on this registration process can be found earlier in this guide book, in the setup section.

Second Screen Setup

If Second Screen is enabled on your Fire TV Stick and you have a Kindle Fire HD/HDX connected to the same local network as the Fire TV Stick, certain applications and media will prompt various notifications and new options on your HDX that you haven't seen before.

For example, when if you install a game to your Fire TV Stick, you might notice a notification like the one above the next time you start your Kindle tablet up. After tapping on the notification and following the instructions from the app app, you can now use your HDX to play part of the game while playing the main game with your Game Controller.

Second Screen isn't just for games, though. With a Fire TV Stick and a Kindle HD/HDX on the same network, you'll notice that—when you go to open a video on your HDX—there's a new icon visible next to the green **Watch/Resume** button:

This icon is the Second Screen icon, and is displayed when you have a choice of viewing your media on your HDX or your Fire TV Stick. After tapping the icon, you'll be shown a popup that looks like this:

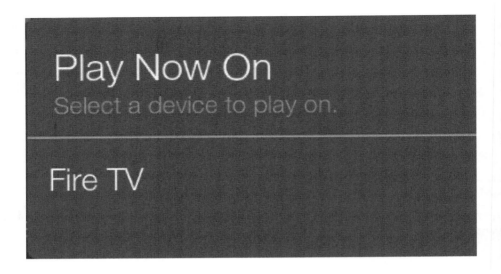

From the list that appears, choose which Fire TV or Fire TV Stick device you want to "fling" the media to. You'll notice that the video will start playing on your Fire TV Stick instead of your HDX. If you want to switch back to playing the video on your HDX, simply tap the Second Screen button again.

And, again, if you want to make the media play on your Fire TV Stick while it's playing on your HDX, just tap the Second Screen button, choose where you want it to play, and boom! It works flawlessly from the testing I've done, and is a fantastic feature for quickly switching between viewing mediums.

Screen Saver Settings

After not being in use for a short period of time (5 minutes by default) your Fire TV Stick will display a series of photos as a screen saver before going into "sleep" mode where the screen goes dark. If you have photo albums in your Amazon Cloud Drive, you can set an album to be used for your screen saver (detailed earlier in this guide). If you don't have any photo albums, or you simply wish to view the included landscape photos on your Fire TV Stick for the screen saver instead, here's how you can do that and more.

From the Home screen, scroll down to Settings, then over to Display & Sounds. Open this section and then open Screen Saver section. Once you do so, the screen saver will start playing in the background of the screen saver options area, giving you a live preview of the screen saver as you change the options around.

In this section, there are several options to explore, which we'll go through now.

Album – Select this option to choose which album to use for your screen saver. If you want to use the included Amazon Collection album, this is where you can set the screen saver to use it.

Shuffle – If this option is turned on, the photos from the album used for your screen saver will be displayed in a random order. If shuffle is turned off, they will be displayed in a linear order.

Slide Style – Use this option to choose what type of transition you want the photos to use when they're transitioning from one to another.

Slide Speed – Adjust the speed of the photo transitions here.

Start Time – Here's where you can adjust how long your Fire TV Stick needs to sit idle before the screen saver engages. This is also where you can turn the screen saver off entirely, by selecting the **Never** option.

Advanced System Settings

Under the **Settings** category and the **System** sub-category are a series of advanced settings and options. You shouldn't have to use or change most of these settings, but just in case you do, we'll go over what they are and what they do now.

About – Shows you details about your Fire TV Stick's name, storage capacity, software version, serial number and more. This section also shows you what network you're connected to, as well as the IP address that's been assigned to your Fire TV Stick. You can also view a total number of remotes/controllers that are connected to your Fire TV Stick here, as well as perform a manual system update check.

Network – This is where you can change which Wi-Fi network you're connected to, as well as configure your wired (Ethernet) connection, if you wish to use that instead of a Wi-Fi network.

Quiet Time – Toggle this option to the On position if you don't want to be bothered by notification sounds. This setting will also hide all notifications when enabled.

Developer Options – If you're a developer creating apps for the Fire TV Stick, you'll want to turn ADB debugging on in this section. If you're not a developer, then don't worry about this section; you shouldn't ever have to mess with it.

Time Zone – Use this option to change what time zone your Fire TV Stick uses.

Legal & Compliance – Filled with lots of boring lawyer-talk, this section is where you'll find the terms of use, safety information, privacy info and other legal information.

Reset to Factory Defaults – Discussed in an earlier section of this guide, here's where you can completely reset your Fire TV Stick to its factory default settings, deleting all of your personal information off of the device at the same time.

Advanced Network Configuration

If you need to change what Wi-Fi network you're connected to, or you want to change from an Ethernet to a Wi-Fi connection (or vice versa), here's how to do it.

From the Home screen, scroll down to Settings, then across to System. Open the System section and scroll down to the Network section. Here you'll see a list of Wi-Fi networks that your Fire TV Stick can detect locally. If you're already connected to one and want your Fire TV Stick to disregard the settings you've input for it, scroll to it on the menu and hit the Menu button on your remote.

If you want to join a Wi-Fi network that's hidden or otherwise unable to be seen by your Fire TV Stick, select the **Join Other Network** option and enter in the SSID, security type and password for the network you want to connect to, and the Fire TV Stick will add this information and attempt to connect to the network.

That's All, Folks!

If you've gotten this far, then you know how to do so many things with your brand new Fire TV Stick! I hope you've learned a lot and that this book has been helpful to you. Don't forget to check out my other books, The Kindle Fire HDX User Guide and Best 100 Kindle Fire HDX Apps. You can find both of these (and more books I've written) on my website at www.CharlesTulley.com.

They're the best resources for learning about your Kindle Fire HDX and finding some of the best apps on the Amazon Appstore to help you be productive and have more fun with your Kindle fire HDX.

If you want to know when updates to this user guide are released and receive helpful tips, tricks and reviews on the latest apps and games, be sure to sign up for the AppSnagr newsletter at www.AppSna.gr/hdxtips and check out the twice a week updates on AppSna.gr and BookSna.gr, too!

Made in the USA
San Bernardino, CA
20 June 2016